Baby raccoon sleeping in hand of CROW staff member

Book design by Craig Keith and Brian Johnson
Cover design by Craig Keith

Photographs by Dr. PJ Deitschel, CROW staff and volunteers, and Brian Johnson

Printed by Direct Impressions, Cape Coral, Florida

To contact publisher, write to islandscene1@comcast.net

ISBN: 978-0-615-24356-6

AMAZING ANIMAL STORIES FROM CROW

Clinic for the Rehabilitation of Wildlife
Sanibel Island, Florida

BRIAN JOHNSON

To Ronel + Christine,
Wonderful
to meet you
down here—
look forward
to seeing you
again!
Best,
Brian + Beth

3

Stories originally appeared in "CROW Case of the Week" in *Island Sun* newspaper

Island Sun

NEWSPAPER
Sanibel & Captiva Islands

for Beth Haely

Table of Contents

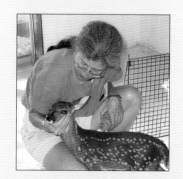

Welcome to CROW...

Things have happened at CROW since 1968.

What started as a makeshift field hospital out of islander Shirley Walter's home is now a critically-acclaimed wildlife rehabilitation clinic situated on 12 acres on Sanibel-Captiva Road.

At first Walter and a handful of residents paid for food and supplies on a shoestring budget. Forty years later CROW, led by co-chairs Bob Wigley and John Schubert, ran a successful $2.8 million dollar capital campaign to finance a new hospital, education center, and student housing complex.

In the beginning CROW was known only by word of mouth, but these days media such as *Animal Planet* and *Martha Stewart Living* have taken CROW to an international audience.

Dr. PJ Deitschel treats loggerhead sea turtle in surgery room

In the 1960s wildlife rehab was regarded by many as an eccentric hobby; now wildlife veterinary medicine is mainstream American culture, and there exists, around the U.S., a network of full-time hospitals and a growing body of wildlife medical research and literature. CROW, with two full-time vets and an impressive track record of rehab success, is widely regarded as one of the best clinics in the country.

CROW is located across from the "Ding" Darling National Wildlife Refuge, a pristine swath of mangrove waterways, West Indian hardwood hammock and colorful birds such as the Roseate Spoonbill and Great Blue Heron. The clinic treats over 4,000 wild mammals, reptiles and birds each year, and they release over half of them back to the wild. The large majority of their patients (approximately 90%) come from off the island -- from Cape Coral, Fort Myers, Pine Island, Alva, Bonita Springs, and beyond. CROW is Lee County's only wildlife hospital.

Most of the animals are injured by contact with human beings; automobiles rank as the number one cause, followed by fishing hooks and monofilament line. Island officials and residents have taken increasing measures to protect the native wildlife by 1) posting signs urging cars to slow down, 2) providing monofilament receptacles at fishing areas, and 3) offering educational programs about wildlife rehab. Individuals

Aerial of CROW property

photo by Jim Anderson

can help save wildlife by driving more carefully and picking up loose fishing line and tackle (see How to Help Wildlife chapter on page 82).

As former CROW board member Steve Brown often pointed out, none of the hospital's patients arrive with health insurance. Nor does the clinic receive any local, state or federal funding. The clinic has remained open since the 1960s almost exclusively because of private donations from individual islanders and other Southwest Florida residents.

In the past decade CROW has upgraded its outdoor caging by adding a sea turtle complex (co-opted at times by water birds such as loons, not to mention alligators), an otter complex, and a mammal compound constructed with recycled plastic and welded wire to facilitate disease control.

The new visitor education center gives the clinic a state-of-the-art reception center for visitors to complement "Ding" Darling and the Bailey-Matthews Shell Museum. Visitors will find exhibits, films, interactive displays, a deluxe gift shop and live footage of a select number of animals in their outdoor enclosures.

CROW's mission is to return wild animals to the wild. As such, they do not keep permanent residents as education "tools" and the hospital strongly discourages people from keeping wild animals as pets. "Freedom," says CROW Veterinarian Dr. PJ Deitschel, "is the greatest gift wild animals possess."

Great Blue Heron with wrap

American Bald Eagle

Rescued:
October 20, 2003

All Michael Orchin knew, as he sped along the Coral Oaks Golf Course in Fort Myers, was that he was supposed to try to rescue a "large bird." As the golf cart came to a stop on the first fairway, he could see the report was correct – for there, standing beside a tree, was an American Bald Eagle.

Fortunately for all parties, Orchin was more than just a volunteer bird lover. Over the years he had rescued all kinds of raptors, and had even engineered a special technique for handling eagles. His method was to cut eye holes in a bed sheet and then approach the bird from behind the linen.

It was a fantastic idea: the eagle never suspected it was a person advancing behind the bedding, and found himself folded up and heading for CROW before he had a chance to get away.

But on this occasion, on the open lawns of the fairway, Orchin had no cover and was spotted right away by the nation's symbol. She was grounded by her fractured right wing, but she could move surprisingly quickly on foot.

The raptor said goodbye to Orchin and ran off. "She was flapping her good wing, and covering a lot of ground," he said. "I couldn't just tackle her or I would have injured her more. I'm sure to the casual observer a 5'11", 240-pound man trying to catch an eagle was a ridiculous sight."

The chase proceeded to a small lake off the fairway, where the eagle plunged in. Orchin did not break stride, but dove in after her. "She made a big mistake thinking momentarily she was a duck," he said. "The water hindered her mobility, and I caught up with her by the time she reached the far bank. As she frantically tried to haul out, I threw the sheet over her and contained her wings and feet. As soon as her eyes were covered she became docile."

Golf course staff went over to assist a soaking-wet Orchin. "When I got out someone mentioned that gators live in the lake," he said. "I had thought about that halfway, but I was already committed."

Orchin placed the eagle, securely wrapped, in the backseat of his car and

Bald Eagle resting on perch in outdoor cage at CROW

drove to CROW. "It was certainly a thrill to hold this magnificent bird in my hands, though I would have liked it to have been under better circumstances," he said.

CROW staff put a hood on her and gave her pain medication and arnica, a homeopathic remedy for trauma. A radiograph revealed a closed fracture of the coracoid, a bone that runs from the shoulder to the chest.

Ready to get back to the wild

It was not clear how the eagle had been injured, but Deitschel suspected from the puncture wounds on her body that she may have clashed with another eagle. Staff placed her in a double-wide cage in intensive care and kept it dark overnight.

"The next day she sat up on her perch and was bright and alert, which was great," said Dr. PJ. "We offered her food, and fortunately she decided to eat on her own right away.

"For the rest of November she stayed very comfortable in a small space. I was hoping she would remain quiet in her cage for five days, so when she hit seven days we were ecstatic, and nine days was awesome. On the 30th we noticed she was becoming rambunctious and trying to peer over the towels covering her cage.

"Obviously there was some concern about her wounds becoming infected, but we did not want to handle her unless absolutely necessary and we could see her wounds well enough to know that there was no infection. Her immune system took care of the problem."

On November 30 staff moved her to the small-flight cage. For the first week she stayed in seclusion in an enclosed section. Then she came out to the main area and experimented with flapping her wings. By December 16 she was able to fly from perch to perch.

After giving her Vitamin B Complex and supplemental calcium, staff transferred her to the large-flight cage. The eagle made several tours of her spacious new compound and seemed to pay for it the next two days because staff reported no further flights.

However, by December 28, she was taking regular and sustained flights around the cage. "Her flights were beautiful and her wings symmetrical," said Dr. PJ. "This bird was picture perfect in terms of how she healed."

The following day Dr. Amber McNamara and Johanna Neil drove out to Coral Oaks Golf Course with Robyn Johnson holding the eagle in her lap. Out on the fairway where she was rescued, the three made a carefully timed release: after McNamara had removed the newspaper crunched up inside her talons, Neil removed her hood and Johnson let her go.

"She flew pretty low down the fairway, turned a corner and disappeared," said Johnson. "We had to thank Michael for turning it one of the more daring rescues of the year."

Readying for the release

Crunched up newspaper in talons

Release at the Coral Oaks Golf Course

Hawksbill
Sea Turtle

Rescued:
June 20, 2008

Ralph Woodring, who was born on Sanibel in 1937 and is the current owner of The Bait Box, rescued a Hawksbill Sea Turtle who had gotten tied up in fishing line behind his home on San Carlos Bay. A boater had alerted Woodring to the sea turtle, and together they hauled her out of water and onto his dock. The turtle had been struggling to get air, but could not get her face above the surface.

Once he pulled the rarely-seen hawksbill out of the water, Woodring tilted her upside down and squeezed her and water flowed out of her lungs. "I don't know if it was the right thing to do, but it worked," he said. "She was a lucky girl, she nearly drowned. A couple more minutes and that would have been it."

There was a hook in her left flipper and monofilament around her body. Woodring let her rest on the dock and watched to see how she was doing; she continued to gurgle up water as she lay flopped on her stomach. "After twenty minutes she started to crawl a little bit so we knew she would probably be okay," said Woodring.

Woodring, a lifelong fisherman, has been one of the leaders on Sanibel urging fisherpersons to clean up their hooks and loose line. He said it is important "to bring it to the minds" of people fishing so they will be more aware of what can happen to wildlife when they come across monofilament. His wife, Jean, said their dog has been stuck by a fishing hook, and she remembers seeing an Osprey who nests near their home flying around with line dangling from his wing for a couple days.

Jean Woodring took the exhausted sea turtle to CROW, where the staff admitted her and examined her condition.

"She had a fair amount of barnacles and organic debris on her shell," said Dr. PJ Deitschel of the juvenile, 5.8 kilogram turtle. "There were fresh scratches under her left arm. She was quite dull and stayed on the

Hawksbill Sea Turtle on exam table

scale when we weighed her without any activity or energy. This was the first time I had seen a hawksbill in my 12 years here at the hospital."

Staff took her to the reptile room and placed her on the soft netting of the loon trampoline and lowered her into the tub. The water woke her up and she became "feisty" and gurgled up more water from her lungs. In the heated room, surrounded by other reptiles, the sea turtle was back to life and looking alert a few hours later.

The following day staff took the hawksbill to the 900-gallon salt water tank in the sea turtle complex. She was delighted with the chance to swim. "As soon as we put her in the tank she dove and swam around," said Dr. PJ. "She looked just fine."

The hawksbill spent the night in the tank, and the next morning Dr. PJ and sea turtle technician "Cat" Turner evaluated her together. They decided there was no reason to keep her: her basic health was sound, and her wounds superficial. On June 23 they took the hawksbill back to San Carlos Bay.

Swimming in salt water tank in sea turtle complex

Baby Mallards

Rescued:
May 31, 2008

The students at Pinewood Elementary in Estero were given an assignment: create stationary with pictures of an endangered animal species for use as a fundraising tool. At completion their teacher asked them who they wanted to donate the money to so they took a vote. The beneficiary of their generous $500 gift? The Clinic for the Rehabilitation of Wildlife on Sanibel Island, nearly an hour north of their hometown.

So, to show their appreciation, CROW Veterinarian Dr. Amber McNamara jumped in her car and headed for Estero to meet with the kids. A couple miles past the Sanibel Causeway, as she approached Shell Point Retirement Community, McNamara spied a line of ducks crossing four-lane Summerlin Road. She slowed down and pulled into the left turn lane as trucks and other vehicles whizzed past her. The mother duck and her ducklings scattered as they felt the wind and roar of the cars sweep toward them, the mother narrowly escaping with her life. "Mom was three inches from being hit," said McNamara.

Some of the ducklings headed back toward the Shell Point side of the road while the others scooted onto the grassy median. McNamara got out of her car and started to track them down, one by one. "They were tiny – the size of your palm," she said. "I could not see them well, they kind of blended in, but I could hear them cheeping."

Going more by sound than by sight, she plucked five of them from the area, putting each one in her shirt. She's not sure, but she thinks she got them all. "They were wiggly, but they seemed to calm down when they felt one of their siblings next to them," said McNamara. The mother she did not see again.

Back at the car, she wondered what to do. "Now I have five babies in my shirt and I'm starting to run late for the presentation," she said.

"So I dumped out the CROW magnets and other items I had in the boxes for the kids, and put the chicks in and closed the top."

McNamara continued to Pinewood Elementary, stopping en route at South Trail Animal Hospital, a traditional drop-off for CROW.

Dining on mash chow in clinic's bathtub

The students were delighted to hear about McNamara's adventurous rescue, though concerned about the mother duck. "The kids were great – they really seemed to care about wildlife and wanted to know what they could do to help. After I told them about the ducklings they all had a story to tell, what animal their Dad found, what animal their Mom found..."

McNamara accepted their $500 donation, thanked them, and headed back to Sanibel. She called the clinic to see what had become of her ducklings and found they still needed to be picked up so she detoured to South Trail and got them.

At CROW the babies spent the first few days in an incubator with a rolled up towel serving as a nest. Staff put a mirror in with them to help prevent habituation to humans. They soon moved to a cage on the main floor of the clinic, where they spent most of the time huddled together and munching on Poultry Crumbles, a chow mash. The highlight of their day was the trip to the bathtub, where they bobbed in the shallow water. "The great thing about baby ducks is that if you give them the right stuff they know just what to do," said McNamara. "We put a heat lamp over the tub to keep them warm, and they get a chance to splash around and clean up."

Gradually staff raised the water level to give them more of a challenge and a larger aquatic environment.

On Day 17 the ducklings went outdoors to the Roberts Cage, where they played in the pool. Staff added greens and cut fish to their mash diet, and over the next month they plumped up and their flight feathers grew in.

By Day 40 they reached the final stage: a trip to the small-flight cage to see how well they could fly. The ducklings passed the aviation tests and were all released on Day 51 to the Iona area, a more secluded section of Fort Myers, with a number of lakes, just a couple miles from Shell Point.

"Hopefully the mother is still in the vicinity and will be able to see them again," said McNamara.

Enjoying a bath

Bobcat

Rescued:
May 20, 2005

Ray Paton lives out in Alva in the Florida countryside, in part, because he likes the chance sightings of wild animals. One afternoon he was amazed to see a 6-week-old bobcat walk onto his porch.

Paton, who said he raised bobcats and wolves in Michigan, resisted the temptation to keep the wild creature as a pet. "I decided to call CROW, and I'm glad I did," he said.

The bobcat weighed 900 grams, or about two pounds. "She was quite young, though she had her little teeth coming in and her eyes were open," said Dr. PJ.

She was thin and underfed, but otherwise seemed in pretty good health. Staff placed her in a double-wide cage on the top floor of the clinic, far from the other animals, and started her on a diet of milk, frozen mice and chicks. "The kind of food," said Dr. PJ, "mom would bring home."

With no fractures or major injuries to treat, the challenge before CROW was to find a way to raise the baby in captivity and keep her wild. Dr. PJ called around the state of Florida to see if any other rehab center had a baby bobcat, but no luck.

"Our goal was to cut down on the human contact as much as possible," she said. "We decided "Cat" Turner (staff rehabilitator) would be the main one to care for her, and she would go in once per day to clean and feed and then get out fast."

On May 30 the baby bobcat was transferred to an outdoor cage near the otter complex. In 10 days her weight had jumped from 900 grams to 1.5 kilograms, and throughout her stay at CROW she would maintain a rapid rate of growth.

"When we weighed her the second time we were happy to see her hissing and spitting," said Dr. PJ. "She was wild from the beginning -- she had very good instincts."

Over the next three months the bobcat matured into a powerful juvenile,

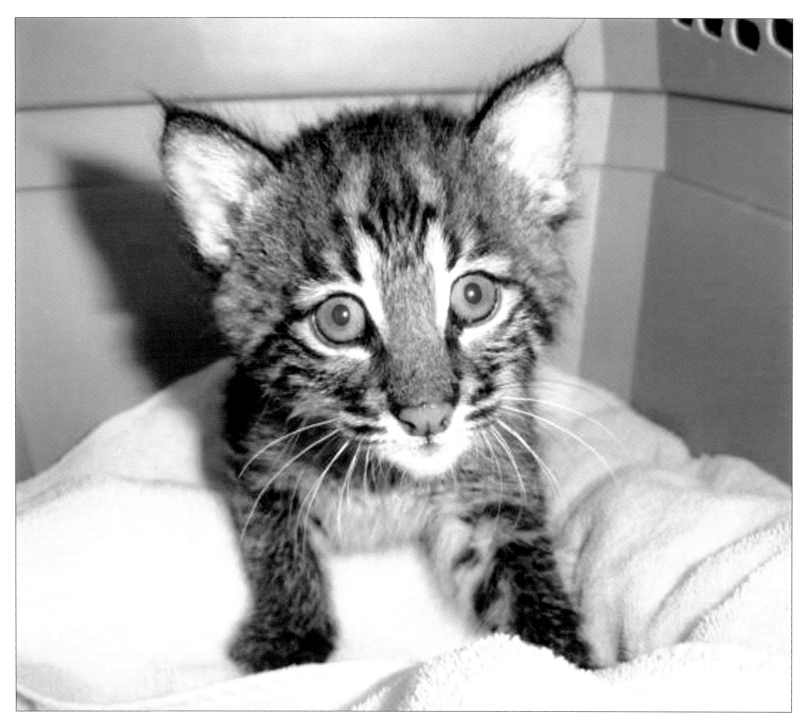

The bobcat looked like a kitten when she arrived in carrier

Exploring outdoor cage

developing her gross motor skills and doubling in size and weight. Although isolated in her outdoor cage, she received frequent visits from bobcats living wild in the area. "This always happens when we get in a bobcat," said Dr. PJ. "Staff saw them hanging around, and bobcat dung outside the cage. The palm fronds on the outside of the cage were torn down."

On August 25 she was moved to the Class II Carnivore Cage, a 28-by14-foot enclosure built strong enough to handle a bear, which gave her more room to run, and the chance to hunt the lizards, mice and rats who wandered unknowingly into her cage.

"At this point we started hiding her food in different objects, sometimes suspending them from the ceiling, to keep her agile and curious and exploring," said Dr. PJ. "They know about hunting without being taught —their instincts are brilliant."

Meanwhile Dr. PJ consulted with other rehabilitators about when to release a bobcat raised in captivity, finding a wide assortment of opinions and theories. She decided to release her at six months, as it coincided with the time juveniles leave their mother in the wild.

In late October Turner drove the bobcat to a property in Labelle with hundreds of acres of habitat. She weighed about 8.4 kilograms, or 20 pounds. It was a classic release.

"She stuck her head out of the carrier and was gone," said Dr. PJ. "She smelled freedom and saw freedom and went for it. She wasn't sticking around – it was a perfect response. I am proud of my staff for keeping her wild...The pictures of her said it all. She came in as a little kitten and left as a bobcat."

Staff kept bobcat wild

One of the more dramatic cases in CROW history involved a flock of White Pelicans rescued from certain death on a wintry lake in Minnesota by retired veterinarian Kent Brunell.

"They got separated from a flock of about 800 White Pelicans who were flying south," said Dr. PJ. "They were found, believe it or not, on Pelican Lake. It was freezing over, and they were running out of a food source. The birds were emaciated when Brunell found them."

The giant white birds were taken to the Wildlife Rehabilitation Center of Minnesota, where they were treated, coincidentally, by Dr. Karen King Shenoy, twice an extern at CROW. Shenoy subsequently sent an email to Dr. PJ asking if CROW could take the White Pelicans once they had been stabilized.

In the meantime, a Minnesota newspaper, the *Star-Tribune*, picked up the story and published a feature article about the rescue.

After clearing a series of bureaucratic hurdles, Dr. PJ emailed Dr. Shenoy and told her CROW would take them. Northwest Airlines charged a discount rate and flew them down to Florida on January 11, 2007.

The anticipation had been building at CROW for their arrival, and there was an excited mood in the clinic as they brought in the carriers. The drive from Southwest Florida International Airport had been easy; getting the agitated pelicans out of their carriers, onto the scale, and then up on the examining table was not.

"White Pelicans are strong," said Dr. PJ. "And you can imagine how they felt being stranded on the ice, going to an indoor rehab center in Minnesota, and then flying in an airplane to Florida. We had to work as a team to handle them."

It took the combined efforts of Dr. PJ, Dr. Amber McNamara, Robyn Johnson, "Cat" Tuner, and extern Pam Cruz to weigh, examine and treat the powerful birds.

"All of them had foot issues, cracking in the webbing and some bumblefoot," said Dr. PJ. "They had been inside in cement enclosures on a

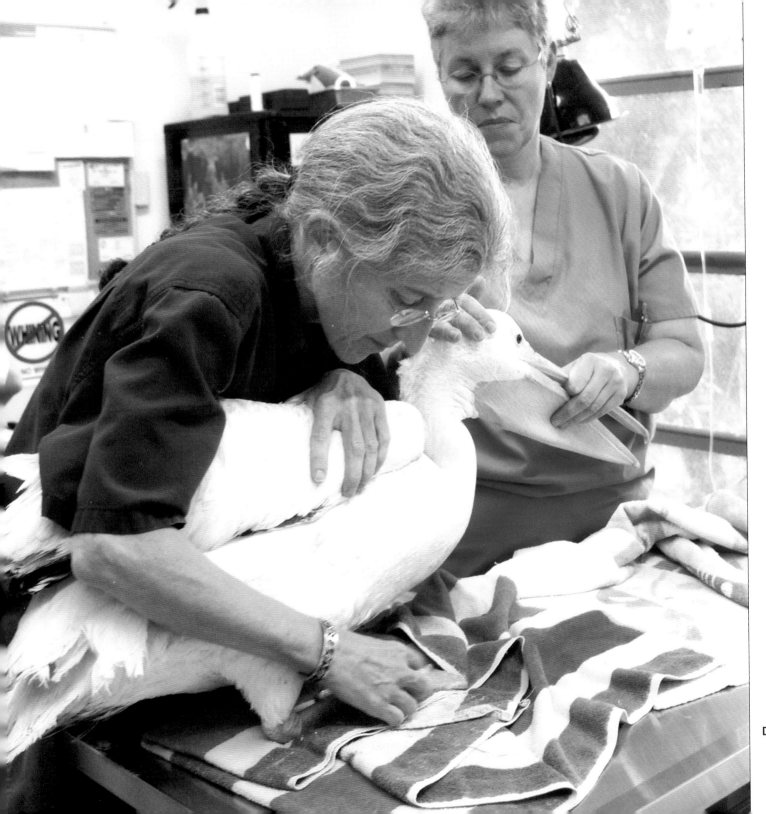

Dr. PJ examines cracked webbing

hard concrete substrate for a month. We are very fortunate here to have access to outdoor cages year-round. We put Boviderm, which is used for the chapped udders of cows, on their feet – it works well for skin problems."

The birds were of varying size and in fair body condition. Their feathers were ratty, but they had no fractures or major injuries. The rehab center in Minnesota had done a fine job treating their frostbite and bruising and bringing them back from the brink of starvation. What they needed now was Florida sunshine and buckets of fish.

After the foot treatments the pelicans were carried, one by one, in the arms of the staff to an outdoor cage with two landing platforms and a pool. Dr. PJ was curious to see how they would interact with the Brown Pelicans, the cormorants and the single White Pelican already there.

"I thought it was really quite spectacular the way they all got along, especially the cormorant who stood right in the middle of them, watching it all," she said. "It was a riot."

The staff enjoyed seeing how happy the White Pelicans were to be in a tropical climate, surrounded by palm trees and a warm breeze. Turner tossed fish into the pool, which they gobbled down, hardly believing their luck. The birds spent the rest of the evening eating and preening and getting to know their cage mates.

The pelicans stayed for one week, basking in the sunshine and fattening up on a continuous supply of fish, going through 25 pounds per day. In a short time their feathers returned to a glossy white sheen.

CROW staff took them to the "Ding" Darling National Wildlife Refuge across the road and let them go into the mangrove estuary, where they soon joined a group of other White Pelicans. "It was quite the story," said Dr. PJ.

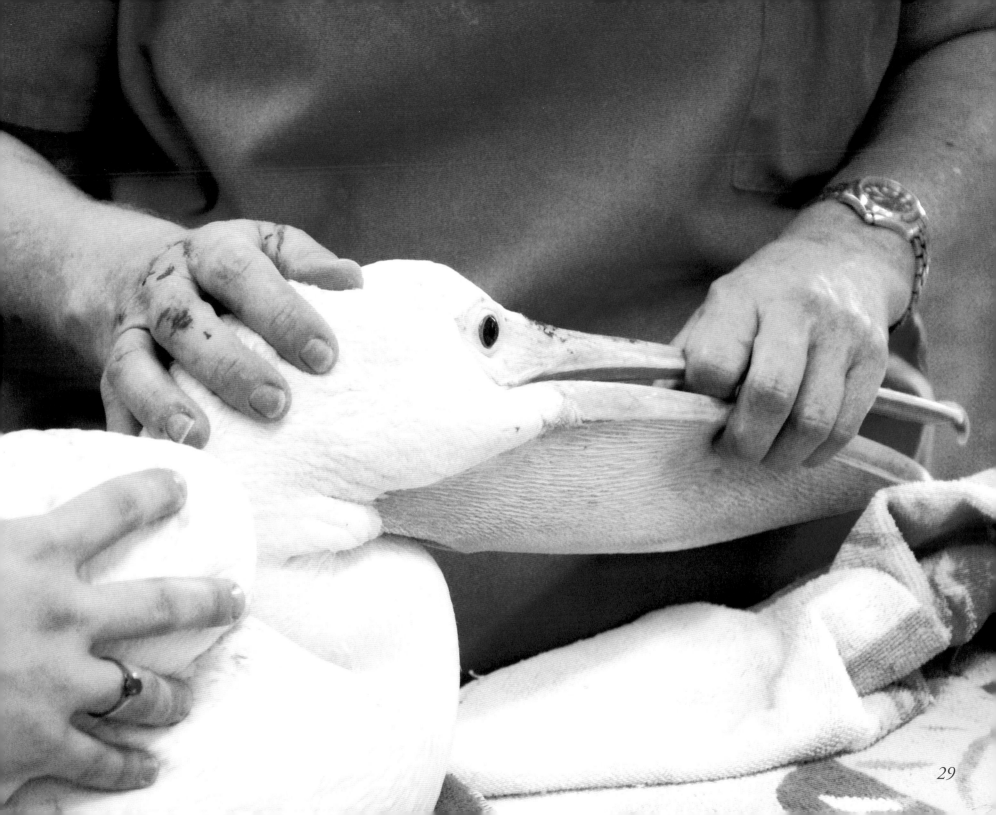

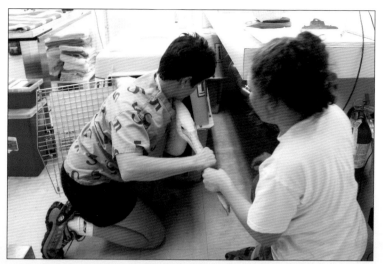

Dr. Amber McNamara and Pamela Cruz pull pelican from carrier

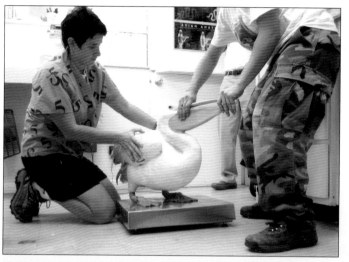

McNamara and Cruz weigh pelican during the check in

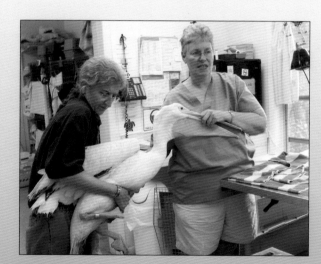

Transferring pelican from scale to examining table

"Cat" rubs Boviderm into chapped foot

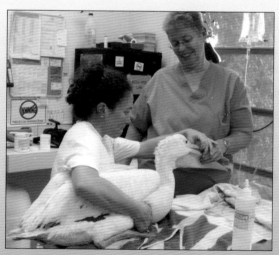

Cruz readies to carry pelican to outdoor cage

The pelicans had an appetite after their flight from Minnesota

"Cat" tosses fish to hungry pelicans

Not letting the fish out of their sight

Robin and Jeff Hurst are living out their own version of the *Swiss Family Robinson* down in Estero, where they dwell on Bamboo Island, a 7.5-acre peninsula that is connected to the mainland by a short bridge without guard rails. It is quiet, feels remote, and is teeming with wildlife.

One morning Jeff was walking out the front door with their dog when he saw something that froze him in his tracks: a 250-pound bear nestled up against the mango tree in their front yard. He got up on all fours when he saw Jeff.

Jeff cancelled the dog walk and backed slowly into his house, like Roy Scheider in *Jaws* when saw the great white shark rise out of the sea at the back of the boat. Inside he called the police and kept his eye on the bear, who later in the morning ambled over the island's rustic bridge and vanished.

Jeff went off to work, and when he came back scouted the area to make sure it was safe for his wife, Robin. As he went to one end of the property he saw a tiny creature on one of the trails. He called Robin by cell phone and asked her to come look.

She knew at once he was a baby River Otter. They looked around the area for the mother, but could not find her. "She was crying a lot, and it was dusk, and we have some big, mean raccoons, so I asked my husband to go back and get one of my old work shirts," said Robin. "As soon as I wrapped her up in the shirts she stopped crying, put her paws over her eyes, and went to sleep." That night she took a couple photos of him in the palm of her hand.

In the morning "Cat" Turner drove half the distance from Sanibel to meet Robin, and brought the tiny, eyes-closed, River Otter to the clinic. Dr. PJ estimated that she was just 5-7 days old, which made her the youngest otter CROW had received in the last 10 years. In fact, they were incredulous when Robin said she had found a baby otter because they usually don't start coming in until the end of January.

"Bamboo Island" otter takes a nap with a stuffed turtle

Dr. PJ and Robin both felt the mother otter may have been spooked by the scent of the bear and dropped the baby while trying to move her from the den.

Staff hydrated her and fed her a milk formula designed specifically for River Otters. The feedings began at 6 a.m. and were given every three to four hours until 9 p.m. At first they tried to use a bottle, but that did not work. "She did not want to suck so we had to tube feed her," said Dr. PJ.

When her eyes opened toward the end of December they put in a mirror so she could take a look at herself and feel she was around another otter. As a species, otters are among the most social. "For them, the more the merrier," said Dr. PJ. They created a play pen for her and gave her several toys.

Robin, a manager at PetCo near Alico Road, kept in touch with CROW to learn how she was doing, and passed the news along to Jeff and her parents, who wanted to follow the case. Over Christmas Robin mailed the otter a play tunnel, toys and other presents.

Otter pups playing in specially designed pool

"On January 24 she was big enough to go outside to the otter complex," said Dr. PJ. "We noticed she was trying to get into her water bowl and swim. While they have great instincts, they usually learn how to swim from their mothers. It's always funny to watch – they stick their face in the water and blow bubbles."

But this otter had no mother or any companions at all, so she had to teach herself. "She was very curious about the water, but nervous," said Dr. PJ. And after two months by herself, she was feeling lonely.

On February 7 CROW received the first baby otter of 2008 when FOX News reporter Eric Pitzi found a baby otter girl in the woods while covering a fire in Cape Coral. Finally, a friend for "Bamboo Island" otter.

"I was waiting to get a sound byte and I saw something out of the corner of my eye near the creek – it was a little black critter," said Pitzi. "As I moved

Smiling under a towel as "Cat" dries her off

closer I could hear this little chirping sound. I thought, What on earth? Then the little girl picked her head up and came crawling toward me. She was cutest little thing. I knew something was wrong for her to do that."

Over the next two weeks in February CROW received two more baby otters from around Southwest Florida. These three housed together indoors while the "Bamboo Island" baby remained by herself in the outdoor otter complex. Fed a virtually unlimited supply of fish, the "Bamboo Island" baby was older and far larger than the other three.

Toward the end of February Dr. PJ felt the little trio were ready for the otter complex. The first meeting was on the comic side. "The three stuck to each other like glue, and wanted to follow her around like she was their big sister," said Dr. PJ. "But she was not sure what to do – she was a little shy."

It was only a matter of time for the ice to thaw. "Within a week she had warmed up to them, and they were all sleeping together in the same carrier," said Dr. PJ. "She's been teaching them how to get into the water and swim. It's a riot to see them. We have video of them playing with the big tire and the golf balls. They move in a mass, like one humongous slinky. When one of them goes on the slide, they all do. They are curious, and constantly playing and rolling in the sand."

In the late spring the group earned their release, and FOX News came out to film them on one of their last days. The crew was surprised at the sight of them. "They were amazed at how big they had gotten and how wild they were," said Dr. PJ.

"Bamboo Island" otter is featured in an exhibit in the new education center at CROW. There are pictures of her arrival, her first meetings with the other otters, and her release with them this summer.

Dr. PJ received a report from the owners of the land a few days after the release. "They saw them in the river and on land – with a big juvenile at the front, and the others following her. 'Bamboo Island' otter may have been little and all by herself at the beginning, but she became the leader of the pack."

The otters immediately took to their release site in the countryside

Raccoon

Rescued:
October 22, 2007

With the kids having a day off from school, Vicki Baker thought it would be fun to drive from their Naples residence to Captiva Island with their friends, the Rolon family.

The kids were starting to get hungry as they wound through the foliage on Captiva Drive en route to the Bubble Room for lunch. Ahead they saw a bright orange school bus stopped in the road.

Vicki put on the brakes, and as they came to a halt, she saw the bus driver looking at a baby raccoon flat out in the road. An ardent wildlife lover with more than one rescue under her belt, Vicki was soon out of the car and at the scene. The bus driver did not see the collision, but he had put a call into CROW.

Vicki did not happen to have a box or towel in her car and wondered what to do. She did not want to pick him up with her bare hands and risk getting rabies or a nasty bite or claw mark, but she felt there was no question she had to do something. "He looked really hurt, and I saw the kids looking out of the window at me with their little faces."

She went back to the car and found the only thing that could serve as rescue equipment – a baby's pull-up. By now, as the cars piled up on Captiva Drive, there was some commotion about the delay. "There was a line of cars behind me, and people were looking at me – it was quite a spectacle – so I put my flashers on. They weren't going anywhere until the raccoon was out of the road!"

Vicki managed to roll the 8-week baby into the pull-up and bring him back to the car. "Mrs. Baker," said youngster David Rolon through the car window, "you're a true superhero."

"That was the best part of the rescue!" recalled Vicki.

The bus continued to remain at a standstill while Vicki pulled over into a driveway on Captiva Drive. Vicki put the raccoon in the shade of a bush, far from the road. Her friend Annie Rolon took pictures, then suggested they go on to lunch.

Vicki Baker uses a baby pull-up to grab raccoon in front of school bus

Baker carries stunned raccoon to side of the road, where family waits for a CROW volunteer

Lunch?

Vicki said they had to keep an eye on the raccoon until the CROW volunteer showed up.

Wait?

Annie suggested they take a vote to see what to do.

The vote was held and the raccoon won a landslide decision, 6-1. "The kids were unanimous," said Vicki. "My friend is afraid of critters, but, sorry... she was outvoted!"

CROW staff member "Cat" Turner arrived shortly and took the raccoon back to the clinic. The Bubble Room was closed by the time the Bakers and Rolons got there, but they found another place to eat.

The baby was in critical condition when he came through the doors of CROW. "There was lots of blood from his mouth and nose," said Dr. PJ. "He appeared to have multiple fractures in his jaw, a split palate, missing teeth, and a fractured bone (humerus) in his left leg. He had an increased respiratory rate and pale mucous membranes."

Staff gave him two different types of pain medication, a sedative, antioxidant vitamins, subcutaneous fluids, antibiotics and the Chinese herb Yunnan Paiyou to reduce any internal bleeding. They put a light splint on his leg and set him in a double-wide cage in ICU.

The raccoon was more alert the next day, but staff watched him very closely, knowing he could take a turn for the worse at any time. "We monitored his vital signs all day," said Dr. PJ. "His breathing became steady with pain medication on board, but you could see his breathing and his heart rate rise as it wore off. In the evening he was looking pale, which was a concern."

Nevertheless, he lived through a second night at the clinic.

On Day 3 staff took a radiograph to see the condition of his leg. It confirmed that he had suffered an overlapping mid-shaft fracture of the humerus in his front leg. This presented them with a medical dilemma: surgery or let it heal on its own?

"We discussed this at length with the externs and other students at rounds – this turned into a great teaching case," said Dr. PJ. "His lungs sounds were rough so he was not the best candidate for anesthesia. But we have treated enough raccoons to know the splint would not last long on his leg – he would start tearing it off."

Feeling "wary" of surgery, Dr. PJ opted for supportive care rather than intervention. "Raccoons, like foxes, are good at protecting their injuries," she said.

By Day 5 the baby was taking in a stream of nutrition in the form of Clinicare, a liquid formula CROW has recently added to their treatment arsenal. "Obviously this little person was agreeable in terms of eating, and this would be key to his rehabilitation," said Dr. PJ.

Staff was pleased to see that his fractured leg was maintaining correct alignment; in fact, he was able to extend his toes, and as he sat on his haunches, it looked perfectly normal. "It was going in the right direction – you could not tell there was anything wrong with it by looking at him."

On Day 14 staff transferred him, after he had pulled apart his double-wide in ICU, to a cage on the top floor. Around this time CROW received a female juvenile raccoon of the same size and age with similar fractures. They were placed in adjacent cages out on the porch.

On Day 31 they moved together to the outdoor stilt cage. "They took to each other like glue," said Dr. PJ. "I'm sure they had all kinds of war stories to tell each other."

Eventually they ended up with a group of several other juvenile raccoons in the woods mammal cage. Both healed their fractures beautifully on their own, gained weight, and developed their gross motor skills. "They became a family unit, and we would not have wanted to split them up after they had bonded, so we released them as a group on January 11. It was a great case."

The Rolon and Baker kids kept asking about the raccoon and they made several calls to see how he was doing. Thanks to them, he made it back to the wild.

Recuperating in an outdoor stilt cage

Cooper's Hawks

Rescued:
May 13, 2008

If you think surgery is complicated, try orchestrating the return of three baby birds back to a nest in Cape Coral. Dr. PJ gives the clinic receptionists top marks for handling daily phone calls, particularly when they involve, as they did in this case, the coordination of an electric company, Cape Coral park rangers, CROW transportation volunteers, pick-up locations, and CROW staff.

"The receptionist job is the hardest job at CROW," said Dr. PJ. "They are answering four phones, fielding emergencies, dealing with people's emotions, directing rescues – everything involved in getting the patients to CROW."

On May 12 CROW received two separate calls about Cooper's Hawk nestlings who had been grounded at Cultural Park Theater in Cape Coral. One hawk baby was taken to Miracle Mile, the other to Kindness East.

They both arrived on the afternoon of May 13. "When we saw the history, and looked at each of them, it didn't take long to figure out they were from the same nest" said Dr. PJ.

The history included sightings of the parent hawks, who had circled the area, upset, when each of the babies had been scooped off the ground and taken away. Dr. PJ asked that day's receptionist, Sue Scott, to start organizing a quick return of the babies to the scene, which might well necessitate an LCEC (Lee County Co-Op)bucket truck.

Meanwhile staff checked the two hawk nestlings for broken bones and signs of internal bleeding. They gave the fluffy white chicks, who were bright and alert, pain medication, fluids and the Chinese herb Yunnan Paiyao. The preliminary exam showed the hawks were in good health, despite their 30-foot drop.

The next afternoon Scott successfully set up an appointment with LCEC to meet a CROW staff member at the Cultural Park Theater. "We have a nice relationship with LCEC," said Dr. PJ. "They're excited to take part in the return of baby birds to their nests, and they have been an extremely valuable partner for us."

Dr. PJ asked handling expert "Cat" Turner to take the hawks back to Cape Coral. She dropped everything and went around the outdoor grounds looking for suitable material for a new nest. The resourceful Turner grabbed palm fronds, pine straw, branches and zipties – and the two hawk babies – and set off for Cape Coral.

Cooper's Hawk nestling in a box at the clinic

That morning a call had come into CROW about a third hawk nestling found in the vicinity. The finder noted that the hawk mother was actually feeding the baby on the ground, which was good news to CROW, as it established that the parents had not left the area.

Tuner and an LCEC worker went up in the bucket to look at the tree while the mother hawk watched them from the nearby roof of the theater. She was surprised when she reached the shattered nest and found a dead hawk chick infested with mites.

The nest itself was in shambles, and Turner surmised that it may have been the parents' first effort at constructing one. Not wanting to contaminate the two live chicks with the mites, she brushed the remains of the nest and the dead baby out of the tree. "The poor little creature – it was the worst case of mites I've ever seen," she said.

Patiently, Turner made a new nest, creating a floor out of the palm fronds and forming sturdy sides out of branches. The LCEC employee assisted her at some of the trickier junctures. The whole time she saw "mama" watching from the roof. Pleased with the finished product, she put the two chicks in it and quickly left the scene.

CROW staff checked out the third hawk baby at the clinic, and the next evening Turner took her home to Lehigh Acres for the night; meanwhile staff set up a second appointment with LCEC at the oak tree for the morning of May 15.

At 7:30 a.m. Turner returned with the third hawk baby, and was happy to see the mother in the nest. She flew across to the Cultural Park Theater as the bucket rose in the air and again watched intently from the roof. Turner was afraid the other chicks might lurch out of the nest from the commotion and the sight of a person, but they stayed in while she deposited the third chick. "I could see them backing up to the side of the nest, so I'm glad I made the walls as high as I did!"

Turner made another fast exit, and the mother hawk soon returned, relieved and astonished, one would think, to have a freshly made nest and three of her babies back.

The little skunk probably never dreamed of the trouble ahead when he crept into a dumpster at the Koreshan State Park campground, located one hour south of Sanibel in Estero, looking for a bite to eat.

"When he tried to exit the dumpster he must have had a plug of food in his belly because he got stuck in the drain hole," said Robert Baker, a ranger for the Department of Environmental Protection.

The spotted skunk had pushed his head and front paws through the opening, but couldn't squeeze the rest of his body through the narrow diameter of the drain hole. Now he was stuck.

Baker climbed into the dumpster to try to push him through, but the skunk was struggling so much that it was impossible to slide him through. The smell of skunk spray added to the already unpleasant odor of the dumpster.

Baker called CROW, where Dr. PJ and intern Dr. Stephanie French were swamped with patients. Dr. PJ concluded that the best plan would be to sedate the animal so he would relax and fit through the opening. This would require a licensed doctor to administer the medication, which would take one of them away from the clinic at a hectic time.

Dr. PJ handled patients at CROW while French headed down to Estero for a rescue mission never diagrammed at vet school. Meanwhile Baker drenched the skunk with olive oil to make him more slippery and shaded his body from the afternoon sun.

Rangers met French at the entrance to Koreshan State Park and escorted her to the site, where she popped into the dumpster and injected the skunk with valium. Within 10 minutes the little creature stopped squirming.

"His back paws were raw from pushing on the dumpster," said French. "Robert positioned the skunk's legs so they were streamlined, and I pulled from the front."

This time the skunk skidded easily through the hole. French gave him a quick exam, put him in a carrier, and drove him back to CROW.

"He was fairly responsive at the clinic considering the stress and trauma," said Dr. PJ. "He had swelling from his knees to his hips, where he had been struggling, and his paws were pretty reddened. His front end looked good. We gave him anti-inflammatories, pain medication and subcutaneous fluids."

With no major injuries, what the skunk needed most was supportive care.

Climbing in the outdoor cage

The following day he ate well, but was sluggish in his cage. "Normally skunks are very, very fast, but he did not lunge or try to escape when we opened the door to his cage," said Dr. PJ.

The skunk spent 10 days on the upstairs porch, eating his fill. The swelling gradually went down and his feet healed nicely. On Day 12 he moved to a large outdoor complex, where he immediately showed off his climbing ability. He was ready for release, but not without a final stage flourish.

Baker volunteered to pick him up and arrived at the clinic in the late afternoon of November 15. But staff could not retrieve the skunk from his cage.

"There is a six-foot log in the cage, and he burrowed himself into it," said Dr. PJ. "There's a little hole at one end, and for a moment we thought he was going to get stuck again! We spent 30 minutes doing everything we could to pry him out, but nothing worked. Finally we put towels around both ends of the log and bungie-corded them down and gave the log to Robert Baker to put in the back of his truck…It's a great story. We can't thank Robert enough. Very few people would have gone to that kind of an effort to help a skunk."

An inquisitive look

Wild Hog

Rescued:
February 25, 2005

Moments after a tiny wild pig was admitted to the hospital, Dr. PJ headed for one of the closets in the clinic in search of play toys. Her first thought was what she could do to keep him from getting bored.

"I'm really fond of pigs," she said. "They are very intelligent and curious. They are not lazy. In fact, the challenge for a rehabilitator is to find enough things for them to do."

The little pig, weighing just 1.5 pounds, had been separated from his mother. Staff noted mild dehydration and discovered a few ticks burrowed into his hide, but otherwise marked him down as healthy.

They took him to a pen on the upstairs porch, where he would get fresh air and hear the sounds of the tropical wilderness. Then the feeding began: he plowed through monkey biscuits, seeds and other high-fat, high-protein meals.

"He had no problem eating what we gave him," said Dr. PJ. "In typical pig fashion he never looked back. He ate everything we put in his room."

The little hog grew before their eyes, putting on five pounds in a matter of weeks. Staff continually rotated the toys in his pen to keep him diverted. When not playing, he sat quietly in what seemed a reflective mood.

Though friendly, he did not like to be picked up, and his squeals startled some of the college-aged externs. "He sounds like he's 200 pounds when he's being handled," said Dr. PJ.

By the middle of March the hog was going on regular field trips to the outdoor cages, where he rooted around in the earth and felt the sunshine on his hide. He liked sitting on the ground, watching lizards and bugs.

At the end of the month CROW transferred the pig back to Alva, a rural area about one hour east of Sanibel, where they had a contact who would assist with his transition into a group of wild pigs. "Wild hog mothers will allow another baby into their litter, and so it didn't take him long to join a new family," said Dr. PJ.

Carried back to outdoor pen after a check-up in the clinic

Great-Horned Owl

Rescued:
December 16, 2006

Because it was the first day of Christmas vacation, Transy Pigott and her three kids had slept in on the morning of December 16. As Transy came downstairs at about 8:30 a.m., she glanced out her back window and saw a dark object suspended on her neighbor's barbed wire fence.

"At first I thought it was a burlap sack," said Transy, who lives one hour east of Sanibel in Alva. "Then as I got closer I saw him move. I said, 'God, please help me help this bird, but don't let me be attacked.' He looked at me with big beautiful eyes, and was taking little steps on the wire below to keep himself lifted up."

The previous Saturday her dog, Molly, had died before she could get her to the vet. She thought of Molly as she approached the owl and hoped this time it would be different.

"I talked to him in a sweet tone of voice to let him know it was okay and I was just trying to help him," said Transy. "He never bit at me, he just looked at me."

She spent 15 minutes at the fence trying to work the Great Horned Owl loose. Her children, Jason, Haley, and Nathan, eventually came out into the yard to see what was going on. She asked them to bring her cell phone and a telephone book. "His feathers had made a knot around the wing, and I couldn't get him free," Transy said. "My husband is a fireman and I knew the guys at the Alva Fire Department so I called the chief and told him what was happening. Well, all the guys on duty came out."

Fire Chief Joey Tiner, his brother Toby, a paramedic and another firefighter arrived at the Pigott property within 10 minutes with gloves, scissors and wire cutters. Transy stayed with the owl until they arrived. "I stood there and talked to him and told him people were coming. I didn't want him to think I had forgotten about him."

The owl's feathers were so entangled that it took the group 20 minutes to pry him off the barbs. Toby held the raptor upright while the others used the scissors to shear away the feathers. They set him on the ground to see if he could fly away, but his wing drooped to the side and he walked around in a daze. Transy handed the firefighters a box with air holes punched in the side, and they placed the owl inside.

After transporting the owl to the Eastside Animal Hospital, Transy took the cover off the box to look inside and see how he was doing. "He just looked up at me, he was so nice," she said. "He knew we were trying to help him."

Dr. Amber McNamara and Robyn Johnson treated the bird at CROW. "He had quite a few wounds on his right wing, and there was a lot of blood matted on his feathers, but it could have been a lot worse," said McNamara. "When I opened the box, his feathers were going every which way, and I thought he must have a fracture, but he didn't. He was lucky because it's easy to get a dislocation when you're hanging from a fence."

Johnson cleaned his feathers and applied the Chinese herb Golden Yellow to his wounds on his wing and right foot. She also gave him the herb Body Sore and pain medication.

"He was dull for three days," said McNamara. "Usually Great-Horned Owls are clacking at you and hissing and have their ears tufted up."

On the fourth night he ate a mouse on his own, and from then on his appetite picked up. Staff moved him to the outdoor Cannon Flight Cage the day before Christmas because he was shredding the towels and newspaper in his cage, a sign he needed more space. On Christmas day he ate seven mice and two chicks.

Over next few weeks he fully recovered from his morning on the fence, and he retained enough feathers to fly. CROW released the Great-Horned Owl back to Alva in the middle of January.

The incredible eyes of a Great-Horned Owl

Yellow Rat Snake

Rescued:
June 18, 2008

Yellow Rat Snake coiled in cage

One summer morning Dr. Amber McNamara arrived at 6:45 a.m., ready for rounds, patient feedings, and the usual routine. There was a box waiting at the front step of the clinic so she peered inside. "There was a little rat snake, maybe two feet long," she said. "She was bright and alert, and there was a little bit of blood. Then I noticed that her heart had pushed out of her body and was beating away."

As extraordinary as it may sound, there is a history of this kind of injury with snakes: a violent collision will cause his or her heart to jettison through the skin and dangle outside the body. "It's really pretty amazing, but we have seen it a few times," she said. "When there is so much force or trauma it can push the heart out."

The rat snake's heart was small – McNamara estimated 2 centimeters – and was drying out in the air. She quickly took the box into the clinic and headed for the surgery room. This qualified as an emergency, to say the least. The externs and fellows soon started to trickle in the front door, and she asked two to help her with surgery; one would handle the anesthesia, the other would monitor a breathing tube inserted in the snake's trachea.

Once the snake was fully anesthetized, McNamara squeezed a drop of saline from a gauze onto the snake's heart to moisten it. Using forceps to open the side of the body wall, she took the snake's heart in her fingers and gently put the beating organ back into place.

"It's a little bit scary," she said. "One slip with the instrument can be fatal – there are so many vessels around the heart. But once I tucked her heart back in, it went to the right position by itself, and the skin came right back together."

McNamara sewed up the area with 3 sutures and they were done. The snake woke up well from the surgery and seemed in good shape. They gave her pain medication and placed her in a warm and balmy reptile aquarium on the top floor.

The little snake did beautifully. The incision healed well, and she became so active by the end of the week that she was promptly released.

Lynne Wilson works at Florida Fitness and Rehab in North Fort Myers, where she treats patients on an outpatient basis. Nearby, in the fields behind the local Publix, lives a flock of Sandhill Cranes.

Cranes are enormous and curious birds, and they are not afraid to investigate human settlements. One of the fire stations in North Fort Myers, for example, often receives visits from these magnificent birds, and a firefighter there once brought one in to CROW.

This habituation to people often brings them, unfortunately, into harm's way. Wilson reports that the cranes behind Publix like to drop in for visits in the grassy area near her rehab clinic. One in particular made repeated appearances. "He had been hanging around the grassy area and walking on the sidewalk," said Wilson. "He would let people get within 4 feet of him before moving away. Our patients would come in the front door and say, 'Hey Lynne, your crane's out front.'"

Although Wilson and the staff at the clinic had become fond of the crane, they did not encourage the visits, knowing it was not in the best interests of the bird – but there was not much they could do to prevent it.

On June 18 one of their patients, on arrival, announced that the crane appeared to have been hit by a car. There were feathers on Route 41 and blood on the crane's wings.

Wilson called CROW and a volunteer was dispatched for the pick-up. Afraid the crane might wander off, Wilson grabbed a sheet and took a staff member with her into the parking lot. They stretched the sheet to its full-length and began to steer the bird to the clinic, where a physical therapy student was holding the door wide open.

"I couldn't believe it," said Wilson. "He was real, real calm and just walked right into the clinic."

They herded him into a bathroom and turned off the light. There were no

Paying a visit to Florida Fitness and Rehab

Walking around the neighborhood near Publix

other rehab patients in the building. The CROW volunteer soon arrived and took the bird to Sanibel.

Dr. Amber McNamara admitted the crane at CROW and found him to be in fair body condition with matted blood, bruising, abrasions and ratty feathers. Dr. McNamara did not palpate any fractures. Staff gave him pain medication and fluids and put him in the largest cage available in ICU.

"The good news," said Dr. PJ, "is that the next day he was standing up and looked bright, alert and responsive."

Like the Great Blue Heron, the Sandhill Crane can't stand fully upright in a CROW indoor cage, so the first priority was to get him outside as soon as possible. The staff gave him a meal to see if he felt well enough to eat, and he devoured it in seconds. In the wild cranes eat an assortment of bugs, grains, and fish.

Staff moved him to an outdoor flight cage, where he regained his strength and healed his injury at a relaxed pace. He did not frantically bang against the netting or refuse to eat, as some large birds do in captivity. However, staff carefully monitored him to watch for signs that he was "ready" for check-out.

On June 22, his fifth day at CROW, he started climbing up the walls and looking for an escape. Staff took him to the large-flight cage, where he successfully made a few aerial maneuvers. Dr. PJ saw no need to delay, and sent him back to the flock behind the North Fort Myers Publix.

"I was talking on the phone with a patient who was mad about their bill so I missed the release," said Wilson. "But we're real excited that he's okay. He came by today, and he had another bird with him. They say they mate for life."

The radiant coloring of the sandhill crane

Brown Pelican

Rescued:
March 4, 2006

The McGowan family, vacationers on Sanibel Island since 2002, were walking the beach near King's Crown condo complex when they saw a Brown Pelican, in the midst of approximately 50 other pelicans, flailing around on a branch in an Australian pine. She was not caught in fishing line but appeared to have gotten enmeshed in the numerous branches of the tall exotic pine tree.

They watched, wondering what to do. The kids, Ginny (10), Quinn (8) and Grace (5), pointed up at the tree, trying to see what was happening.

"Whenever we are at home in Chicago it seems that we come upon a stray dog and take it to the police department – they're real animal lovers," said Mike McGowan, their father. "The poor thing was flapping away, and some of the beachgoers said she had been doing that for a couple of hours. We were worried that she was either going to crash onto the ground or perish up there."

Mike's wife, Karen, made several calls but couldn't get through to anyone so Mike returned to their condo at Sand Pointe and placed a call directly to CROW. The receptionist coached him through the technique for catching a Brown Pelican, telling him to approach from behind and throw a towel over the bird's head. She explained that when controlling the beak he had to be careful not to suffocate the bird.

When Mike returned the pelican had fallen to the ground and somehow managed to shuffle into the shade of the King's Crown buildings. "Just as we were about to execute the plan a CROW volunteer showed up," he said. "I was kind of excited about saying I put my hand inside the beak of a pelican, but it was nice that she came. She handled it like a pro."

The volunteer took the 3-kilogram bird to the clinic, where she was examined by the staff. "The pelican was dull, but at least responsive," said Dr. PJ. "She had an increased respiratory rate and was somewhat shocky, but no internal injuries. She had a shoulder droop from the struggle."

Staff gave her pain medication and fluids and put her in a quiet cage for the

Enjoying the warmth of the heat lamp

rest of the day. In the morning they administered the Chinese herbs Body Sore and Yunnan Payiou, vitamins, and anti-inflammatories. "All in all she looked pretty good," said Dr. PJ "We've seen birds survive falling some incredible distances."

She stayed at CROW for four weeks, and the supportive care allowed her injured wing to heal by itself.

The McGowan family was thrilled with the news of the successful rehab. "We're happy for the Brown Pelican," said Mike. "My family loves Sanibel to death. My kids keep saying at bedtime that they wish they were down there! Every year we celebrate Grace's birthday on Sanibel, because it falls on spring break."

Relaxing behind the bath curtain

Kemp's
Ridley
Sea Turtle

Rescued:
September 17,
2003

Terry Doyle, a wildlife biologist at the 10,000 Islands National Wildlife Refuge, was on his way back from a shorebird survey when he saw a sea turtle floundering in the water east of Marco Island.

Doyle often catches glimpses of sea turtles while out in his U.S. Fish & Wildlife Service boat, but only for a moment. "Typically they dive when a boat approaches," he said.

But this one, a 25-pound juvenile Kemp's Ridley, was flopping around and struggling to breathe as Doyle passed by – so he turned the boat around.

Just as he pulled close to the creature, she gave a last burst of energy and dove below the boat. "I thought, "Oh, man, this sea turtle is in distress, but not enough distress for me to catch her," recalled Doyle.

However, the Kemp's Ridley was wiped out when she came back to the surface, and he easily leaned over and hauled her into the boat. He pulled into port, washed her off with a hose, situated her in the back of his vehicle and drove her all the way to Sanibel Island.

"She was pretty dull when she came in," said Dr. Amber McNamara. "She could hold her head up a little and had a full blink, but she could not do much else. She was just exhausted."

Staff placed her in a shallow baby pool inside the clinic so she could rest and not struggle to stay afloat. A radiograph was taken, but no foreign bodies such as hooks or plastic bags were found in her stomach.

"However, her lungs were more dense in the radiograph than they should have been, so we put her on antibiotics to treat a possible infection," said McNamara. "We did see a ton of shells and crab legs in the GI tract, so we knew she had been eating well."

Her body condition, in fact, was quite good. Her only visible defect was a notch missing from the periphery of her shell (near her feet), an accident that had occurred long ago.

Staff kept her inside the clinic for two days because she was so weak.

"The next day she was stronger and shifted off her stretcher into the water, but it was an effort for her to come up to breathe," said McNamara. At first she swam about frantically in the tank, trying to escape.

On Day 5 she adjusted to the tank, resting on the bottom and casually floating to the top for air. She looked so good that CROW allowed her to stay in the tank overnight by herself.

"From that point on she made a great turnaround," said McNamara. "She didn't want the frozen fish we put in with her, but she gobbled up the live shrimp. After clearing up her infection, we didn't have to do much for her except give her a place to rest and eat."

Three weeks later CROW returned her to the 10,000 Islands; Doyle was ecstatic. "These waters are an important place for these turtles to live during their sub-adult life," he said. "It's pretty cool to put her back here. It feels like I've accomplished something – the Kemp's Ridley is the most endangered of all the sea turtles."

Taking sea turtle on board for release

Staff can feel sea turtle's excitement as she goes over side of the boat

Reaching for the water

Back into the 10,000 Islands!

Red-Shouldered Hawk

Rescued:
April 28, 2008

As time goes on, Dr. PJ sees more that she likes about acupuncture, one of the most potent instruments in the clinic's Eastern medical kit.

The patient, an adult Red-shouldered Hawk, was rescued by Robert and Lylette MacDonald, who noticed him in their Fort Myers yard in the morning and then in the afternoon. They grabbed the listless bird and took him to CROW.

"He was extremely dull, dehydrated and thin," said Dr. PJ. "He weighed only 365 grams, which is quite low for a Red-shouldered Hawk. His eyes were closed, and both wings drooped. He was very, very weak."

Yet the bird was alive enough to know during his exam that he was being handled by human beings, and he reacted with respiratory distress. The staff had to move quickly with their diagnostics to keep him from "going over the edge."

Staff gave him oral and subcutaneous fluids, a homeopathic detox spray and put him in a quiet cage. "We suspected a toxin or some bacterial or viral disease," said Dr. PJ.

The blood work revealed severe dehydration, though his packed cell volume and protein count came back okay.

The next morning the bird was a little more alert, but still had no blink. He had built-up discharge in his sinuses and mouth. "There was something in his crop that was not digested," said Dr. PJ. "He had severe Qi stagnation."

On April 30 he took a turn for the worse – he was extremely dull and laid flat out in his cage. Staff added the Chinese herbs Four Gentlemen and Happy Earth to help support his GI tract.

The bird was no better on May 1, had not eaten since his arrival and hovered somewhere between life and death. With the hawk lying on his chest, Dr. Amber McNamara decided to try a round of acupuncture.

She found three points, including "Kidney 1," which is located in the pad of the foot.

CROW staff wishes they had a film of what happened next. "The hawk literally lifted his head and stood up," said Dr. PJ. "I've never seen anything so dramatic here at the clinic."

The bird stood for the rest of the day and suddenly had an animated look. They left a mouse in his cage that night, wondering if he might take it on his own. In the morning the mouse was gone.

"From that point on, this was a different bird," said Dr. PJ.

By May 4 he was eating well enough to transfer to a double-wide cage upstairs, and on May 9 they moved him to the small flight cage. He was flying around with so much energy on May 11 that they released him.

The hydration and the supportive care were vital, but it was the acupuncture that seemed to have had the punch needed to restore the bird to life.

"We've seen enough good results from Chinese medicine to truly believe in it," said Dr. PJ. "It's a wonderful addition to the Western medications and technologies we use at the clinic."

With the support and backing of the CROW board, Dr. PJ enrolled at the Chi Institute in 2003, and spent numerous weekends over the next nine months learning about Chinese medicine. She has found it to be particularly effective at treating the spinal trauma of gopher tortoises and the toxicosis of birds.

"I absolutely loved it," she said. "It's a complicated but beautiful system. To me, it makes a lot of sense – I relate to it…when we do presentations, I get more questions about it than anything else, and no one has scoffed at it. People are interested."

An acupuncture treatment may have saved the bird's life

Raccoon

Rescued:
August 29, 2002

Janice Fassett was working in her yard when the heavens opened and a baby raccoon fell to the earth. "I was out doing some cleaning by the water faucet when I heard something hit the tin roof," said Fassett. "Then it rolled off and hit me in the back of the neck! I had no clue what it was. I looked down and there was a little raccoon!"

Fassett was worried about how he had taken the fall so she picked him up gingerly and put him in a basket. He was so young that his eyes were still closed. He weighed 172 grams, not much more than a newborn.

Fassett wondered how he fell out of the sky. She looked around her property, but no trees hung over her roof. The only reasonable explanation was that a bird, probably a raptor such as hawk or an osprey, had dropped the raccoon out of his talons by mistake.

When the CROW staff heard about the story and thought about his close call, they felt an extra bond of affection for him. "He's the luckiest raccoon in America!" said "Cat" Turner.

Generally Dr. PJ doesn't like to give CROW's patients nicknames because she regards them as wild animals, not pets, but in this case she couldn't say no to the staff: they dubbed him "Gravity."

Amazingly, "Gravity" seemed unharmed by his adventure. Dr. PJ could find no fractures or puncture wounds or signs of internal trauma. He was just a little dehydrated.

Over the following few weeks CROW gave him standard baby care, feeding him a raccoon milk formula. On September 23 they moved "Gravity," whose weight had jumped from 172 to 1,250 grams, to a small enclosure outside with other orphans.

"The stilt cage introduces him to the sounds outdoors," said Dr. PJ. "It's not a tall cage so there is no chance of him falling and hurting himself."

His experience with the raptor and the tin roof had not made him afraid of heights, and he developed his climbing skills at the normal rate. Raccoon babies normally stay with their mother for four months, so CROW kept "Gravity" until the end of November, when they released him back to the wild, much too large to be picked up by a hungry bird.

"Gravity" stretched out on a cage on top floor of clinic

Marsh Rabbit

Rescued:
May 13, 2008

Romeo saw something hobbling in the grass in the early morning. Margarethe Miville followed her dog through their backyard in Captiva, wondering what he had found. Romeo sniffed the terrified Marsh Rabbit, but did not bite him.

Margarethe scooped up the creature at once and took her inside. "I knew something was wrong because she was running so slow – wild animals are usually very fast," she said. "And I knew she was hurt because she was missing fur."

It was just past 6 a.m. and her kids were still sleeping. She put the rabbit in a box with some paper tissue and placed her in the dark under the stairwell while she prepared breakfast for the family and got everyone ready for the day.

After the kids got on the school bus, she drove the rabbit to CROW. Margarethe said they have rabbits on their property from time to time, but they scatter during periods when they have a bobcat sighting. "They're such tough little creatures, I don't know how they survive – they leave their mother at such a young age," she said. "I just love them."

The rabbit was disoriented on arrival, with matted blood on her fur and around her mouth. "There was a very large wound across her back and rump, a de-gloving wound, and we noted puncture marks deep into the muscle," said Dr. PJ. "The skin of rabbits tears easily – it is an adaptation that gives them another way to escape from a predator, but makes it difficult to suture."

Staff sought to relieve the pain of the wounds with two types of pain medication and a topical cream; they also gave her antibiotics to ward off infection. The rabbit was put in a carrier in the upstairs rabbit room, one of the most private areas of the clinic.

The first 24 hours would be the most critical, as the rabbit tried to regroup from the trauma of the attack, the nasty wound and the anxiety of being handled by humans. "Rabbits can die overnight from the stress of being so close to people," said Dr. PJ.

The Marsh Rabbit stabilized during her first couple days and was moved to a larger enclosure in the clinic. Soon the remarkable healing powers of the species kicked in. Before the staff's eyes, the large wound shrunk to less than the size of a dime. "It was like the closing of a circle of a stringed purse," said Dr. PJ. The Marsh Rabbit fed well on baby greens and cut hay and was released at the end of May.

Handling wild rabbits is kept to a minimum

Wood Stork

Rescued:
October 29, 2007

One October a mass of Wood Storks visited the lake behind Kathy Cronk's condo at Kelly Greens in Fort Myers. After they departed, one Wood Stork remained behind.

She kept an eye on the bird, and after two days came to the conclusion that something was wrong with her. At first she had been able to fly to the tiny island within the lake, but by October 29 she swooned by the water's edge and could hardly keep her head up. "I thought, this poor thing is in trouble," said Cronk.

Although the flock had left her behind, two Wood Storks returned, apparently to keep her company. "One seemed to encourage her by flapping in the water, and the other sat right next to her…the bill of the Wood Stork is amazing, they are magnificent birds," said Cronk.

She called CROW, and the ailing Wood Stork arrived at the clinic on the afternoon of the 29th. "She was very thin, very dull, and was sitting on her hocks with her beak down on the ground to steady herself," said Dr. Amber McNamara. "She had no blink in her third eyelid – it was all the signs of toxicosis, though we usually don't see it in Wood Storks."

CROW staff began standard supportive care to flush the toxins out of her body, including Ginseng and the Chinese herb Qi Performance, fluids, and injectable vitamins.

The bird continued to lose strength that day. In the morning she looked so inert that a volunteer announced that the bird had died during the night. But the Wood Stork was in fact clinging to life and still breathing.

For the next few days she sat in her cage with a towel over her eyes, not moving, not eating. "On Day 4," said McNamara, "she had a creamy froth coming out of her mouth – not a good sign. I looked at it under the microscope – there was a lot of bacteria. She had an infection in the sinus area."

McNamara started her on the clinic's most potent antibiotic and tube-fed

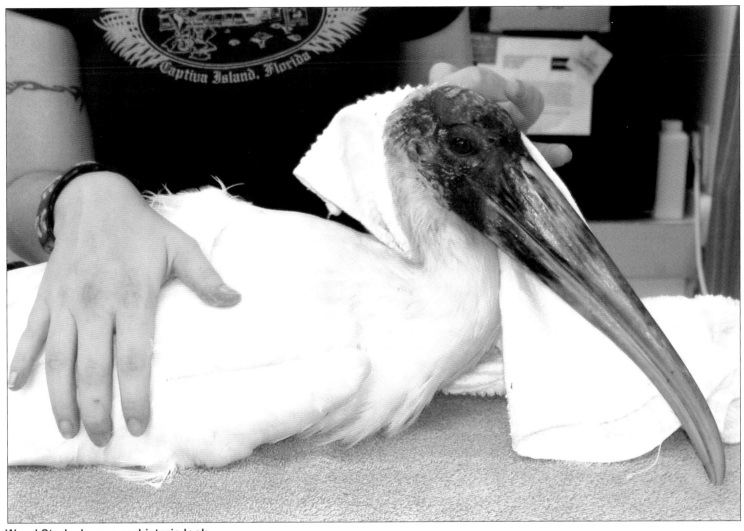
Wood Storks have a prehistoric look

her a fish slurry for desperately needed nutrition.

Day 5 brought the first piece of good news: the Wood Stork managed to climb on her hocks. The staff gave her physical therapy to ward off constriction to her joints and muscles, and continued to administer artificial tears to help her eye-blink woes.

On Day 12 the staff found the Wood Stork standing in her cage. "So we put a finger mullet in with her, and she ate it," said McNamara. "You get so excited, it's hard not to overfeed!"

Four days later staff transferred the prehistoric-looking creature to a larger enclosure inside the clinic. "She was very cooperative with the handling – many of the big birds would have been frustrated by this point," said McNamara.

On Day 21 she looked strong enough to graduate to the outdoor grounds, where she took lodging in Multi-Purpose II. Wood Storks living on the island soon became aware of her presence and stopped by periodically to stand on the top of her cage.

After a week of continuous eating, the bird was ready for the last stage in the transition back to the wild: time in the pelican compound with the outdoor pool and other birds. She did magnificently and was soon returned to Fort Myers.

Wood Stork flock at Kelly Greens residential community in Fort Myers

Hans Raab, a native of Stutgaart, Germany and a true friend to wildlife, noticed a Virginia Opossum lying in a ditch on the morning of January 28 after he dropped his wife, Ilona, off for work. The little animal was not moving, and he thought she must be dead.

"The cars are driving like crazy," he said. "I thought she was another victim."

In the past he noticed a number of mallards killed by cars on Evans Avenue, a busy street in Fort Myers.

Later in the afternoon, when he picked up his wife, he noticed two large black vultures on the side of the road, not far from the opossum. Looking more intently, he saw signs of life.

"Suddenly she moved – that was my signal to rescue her," said Raab. "She was in so much pain, you could see it, you could feel it…I chased the vultures away and went down into the ditch. It was a mess, a little canal with no water in it. I had a box and picked her up. I tried not to hurt her, I was very cautious, because I thought she was already hurt…my wife and I drove immediately to CROW because she was still alive and there was no one to help her."

It was dark at CROW, and the clinic had officially closed, but they saw a student on the dirt road and explained the case. Dr. Stephanie French was soon notified, and she returned to the clinic to admit the Virginia Opossum.

"She was very thin, wet, cold and dull," reported Dr. PJ. "She was a small opossum, the size of a juvenile, but we looked in her pouch and found tiny pinky babies."

They weighed one of the babies and found he was a mere 4.3 grams. "Not as big as a gummy bear, for gosh sakes," said PJ.

CROW staff does a near miraculous job of raising very small babies by hand, but these guys were so miniscule that there would be little hope if the mother did not survive. So the staff put their attention toward saving the opossum mom.

They gave her pain medication, subcutaneous fluids, the Chinese herb Body Sore, and Vitamins A, D, and E. What the opossum appreciated even more was the warm incubator they found for her, which thawed out the chill from the canal.

Weighing in

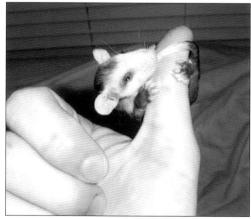

Hanging on

"She had a lot of dirt in her nostrils and ears, and some blood," said Dr. PJ. "But her jaw was intact and she had no fractures. Somehow she did survive the night."

The first 72 hours were touch and go, as the opossum remained listless in the incubator. The babies were all alive, but they would not last long without an active supply of milk. Staff tube fed the mom fluids and a full-nutrition liquid formula called Clinicare.

On Day 4 the mom drank the Clinicare out of her bowl during the night, the first sign that she was on the road to recovery. In a couple of days she began to eat cat chow and egg out of her bowl. The babies gained weight right along with her.

One month later staff moved the mom and her babies to an outdoor stilt cage. The babies ballooned in size, going from 5 grams to over 150 grams by the end of March. They ate so robustly that their mom eventually became irritated with their bouncing all over her and hanging on.

"With seven babies mama got fed up," said Dr. PJ. "She started tearing up the cage. In the wild they start to fall off one at a time at that age, but there was nowhere for them to go – they were all in the one cage with each other. They will hang on for a long time, if they can. We once had a mom come in with two 250-gram babies in her pouch!"

On April 4 the babies were big enough to leave CROW. "The mom looked great, and they looked great, so we released them all together," said Dr. PJ. "It's pretty amazing that we were able to pull her through, and she was able to pull them through."

Raab and his wife were delighted when they got the news. "We had the number to CROW, but I was scared to call because I did not want to hear that she had died or had been euthanized," said Raab. "We did not think she would make it…I'm happy to hear that she survived, that's a happy ending, I like that."

The Virginia Opossum is the only marsupial in Northern America

Yellow
Rat Snake

Rescued:
June 3, 2005

A Yellow Rat Snake arrived who was suffering from an unpleasant meal: the reptile had mistaken two golf balls for bird eggs, and was finding they weren't going down very well.

The snake had crawled into the aviary of a Naples bird fancier and swallowed the appetizing white globes. "Apparently it's quite common when trying to get a bird to lay eggs in a certain spot to use decoys such as golf balls, marbles and light bulbs," said Joanna Fitzgerald, a wildlife rehabilitator who coordinated the snake's admittance to CROW.

Dr. PJ ordered surgery right away to relieve the pressure of the sporting goods against her inner organs. "They had already settled at the bottom of her stomach, and her lungs were unable to expand fully," she said. "We had just been talking at morning rounds about how the body handles foreign bodies such as a small rock or a penny. Sometimes they are regurgitated, but often they pass through. Obviously these two balls were not going to pass through on their own!"

Staff placed the snake in an anesthesia box and prepped her for surgery. Dr. PJ made an incision below the stomach, cutting between the scales rather than through them, a surgical tactic which allows better closure of the skin. The golf balls came out cleanly.

"It was easy to do because the balls had stretched out the area and I knew exactly where to go," said Dr. PJ. "The difficult part was closing it up, which was left to Dr. Amber McNamara. We were sharing the surgery, and she got the tough part."

The snake was in a fighting mood when she awoke. CROW kept her for six days in the heated reptile room in order to provide her with antibiotics and pain medication and check her stitches. They did not feed her.

"The wound was healing beautifully – it was a good, sterile surgery," said Dr. PJ. "But she was not content to be a captive. From the first morning she lay coiled on the top of her box, ready to strike. We might have kept her a little longer to monitor her condition, but she wanted out. She was destroying her enclosure and we didn't want to see her hurt herself trying to escape."

Removing the golf balls

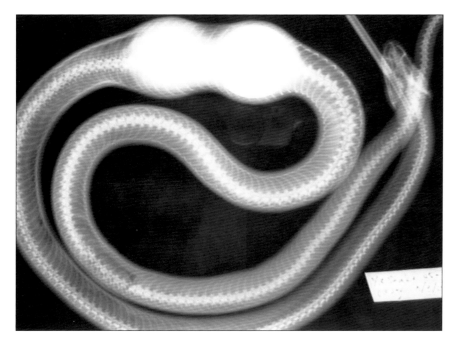

Radiograph reveals the golf balls

Snake prepped for surgery

Shirley Walter

Walter carries a Magnificent Frigate

She felt frustrated.

She had gone to "Ding" Darling National Wildlife Refuge to see if they would care for the Brown Pelican she had seen on the bridge with a broken wing. The bird had been hit by a car and could not fly.

The official she spoke with at the refuge was pleasant enough – it was the information she didn't like: he said they did not give medical attention to injured animals. "There must be someone who takes care of them!" she replied.

Not long afterwards she found two Royal Terns languishing on the Sanibel Causeway. This time she bundled them into her car and took them home.

Now there was someone on the islands who

Barred owls in a picnic basket

would take care of injured animals: Shirley Walter.

"Being kind of an activist, I said, well, someone's gotta do something about it," she recalled during her summer visit in 2007.

Walter's act of service for the two terns – in 1968 – became the start of CROW. Word of her rescue and rehabilitation of the birds spread around the islands, and before she knew it her house had become a Noah's Ark. "I had animals everywhere," she said. "At one point I had 43 pelicans – it was intense at feeding time!"

Walter would throw a cast-net into the water at Blind Pass (near the bridge to Captiva Island) to catch fish for the birds, and also took trips to Miami to get stores of frozen fish. She found a kindred spirit in Dr. Phyllis Douglass, a cat and dog veterinarian who was willing to offer advanced medical treatment for the animals who arrived at Walter's home with complicated injuries. In those days, they sent animals who could not be released back to the wild to Sea World, where they lived as permanent residents.

To most islanders she was a folk hero. But then, as now, there were a few who opposed the idea. Walter had an answer for her critics: "My bottom line was: Man is responsible for 90% of these injured animals, so we are responsible to care for them."

A waterbird and St. Francis behind Walter's home

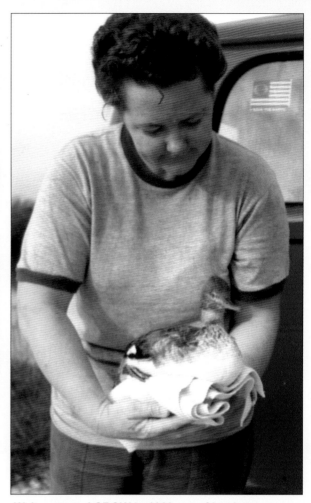

Walter started CROW in 1968 out of her home

Walter used her VW Bug for numerous rescues

Releasing a duck back to the wild

Walter became a strong advocate of educating the public about wildlife rehab. Due to her sustained efforts, CROW became incorporated in 1971 and eventually became an island organization mentioned right along with "Ding" Darling and the Sanibel-Captiva Conservation Foundation.

Walter now lives in Ocala, Florida (almost 300 miles north), but each year, when able, she makes a pilgrimage back to Sanibel for her "CROW fix," which means cleaning cages, feeding the animals and doing laundry. "So much has to be done – there's always a need for help," she said. "It's a good feeling to see the level of care that goes on here. It involves a lot of work."

Walter stays connected to CROW during the year, reading newsletters, following the patient cases and corresponding with Dr. PJ by email. Watching the clinic grow over the years has been one of the great joys of her life.

"I'm happy I was a little part of it in the beginning, and proud of what it's become," she said.

A 2007 visit to CROW to volunteer

Dr. PJ Deitschel & Staff

Dr. PJ named her first rabbit after the famous German physician and missionary, Albert Schweitzer, whose philosophy of "reverence for life" mirrors her own.

"Schweitzer was a man of medicine, music and religion," said Dr. PJ, "but most importantly he was a man of compassion and peace."

While reading about the 1952 Nobel Peace Prize winner, she happened to meet Claske Franck, who had worked with her husband, Fredrick, beside Schweitzer in Africa. Franck gave Dr. PJ a postcard copy of one of her husband's pencil drawings. It pictured Scheweitzer writing at his desk in the African jungle with a line of his "pet" ants marching past him across the table top. For Schweitzer, even the smallest of creatures had inherent value and knowing kindred spirits like the Francks was an inspiration for Dr. PJ.

A "call to service" led Dr. PJ to the field of wildlife rehabilitation--and eventually to veterinary medicine. She took a job in 1985 at Lifeline For Wildlife, a wildlife rehabilitation center in upstate New York , and began to learn the trade.

One day a badly injured, domestic rabbit arrived at the clinic. Dr. PJ cared for the young rabbit, and named him Schweitzer. Later she nursed another rabbit back to health – this one she called Gandhi – and the two rabbits became a bonded pair.

"The writings of Schweitzer and Gandhi have had a strong influence on my life," she said. "What drew me to Gandhi was his call to non-violent confrontation, his belief that intolerance is changed one person at a time."

Dr. PJ brought this spirit – reverence for life and a call to action – to Sanibel when she arrived at CROW in March of 1996 as a senior vet student. Staff and the board of directors immediately sensed the depth of her commitment to wildlife rehab, and she was tapped as the head veterinarian when the position became available in November of 1998.

Dr. PJ gives a gopher tortoise acupuncture

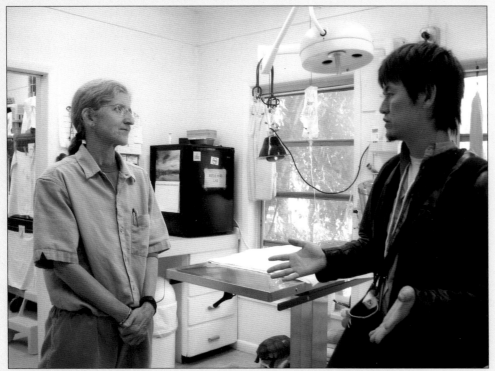
An international audience for CROW: Dr. PJ talks with Japanese cameraman

Since that time Dr. PJ has become something of a folk hero to the eco-minded residents of Sanibel & Captiva. She is frequently asked to speak to local organizations, where her passion and enthusiasm inspire support for CROW's work. In 2005 the Florida Wildlife Federation named her the Wildlife Conservationist of the Year – it marked the first time the prestigious federation selected a wildlife rehabilitator for this award.

"I was very proud for our profession," said PJ. "Our mission at CROW is to keep alive the vision Shirley Walter started in 1968 and this award, in a way, validated all her efforts."

Dr. PJ's approach to wildlife medicine blends East and West: Chinese herbs and acupuncture figure in her treatment protocols as much as antibiotics and orthopedic surgery. She devoutly follows the Hippocratic Oath of doing no harm,

preferring non-invasive treatment whenever possible. She "listens" to her patient's needs and formulates a treatment plan based on the individual. And she delivers the same message to the students who come to CROW from around the world: "All life is unique and every person has value no matter which species they belong to."

Dr. PJ is quick to share credit with the staff who share time in the hospital's trenches, a group that includes Dr. Amber McNamara, Robyn Johnson, "Cat" Turner and Nikki Talianko, and volunteers such as Ann Martin and Bonnie Dale. She gave Anita Pinder, the operations manager at CROW, a glue stick to symbolize her holding the hospital together through various times and seasons. "This is not a job where you punch the clock," said Dr. PJ. "It's a life and a commitment and a belief in Shirley's vision. I feel blessed to have a team that functions as a whole. Everyone leaves their egos at home, and that, I think, is unusual."

McNamara arrived from veterinary school in 2003 for a one-year internship. Dr. PJ was impressed with her talents and offered to hire her on a permanent basis. "I don't know of another vet who is more qualified or competent," she said. McNamara gives CROW a second vet who is licensed and trained in wildlife rehabilitation and Chinese medicine.

Johnson started as a volunteer and eventually found herself putting in four days per week. Her nursing background and love of wild animals led to a full-time position. She has a particular expertise in feeding and caring for baby birds and over the years became Dr. PJ's "right hand person."

Nikki Talianko

Anita Pinder

Ann Martin, Bob Wigley and Ann Moran at groundbreaking for visitor's center

Turner also started as a volunteer and found she too wanted to make wildlife rehab a vocation. Dr. PJ describes her as "fearless" and a go-to person at the clinic to get a difficult job done. "At first I wanted to be a zoo keeper," said Turner, "but after working here, and getting to see the animals go back to where they belong – that's what gives me the most rewarding feeling."

Talianko began as an extern in 2002 and is now, like Turner a staff rehabilitator. A typical day includes cleaning cages, feeding the animals, baby care, and handling patient medications. "I like the environment at CROW," said Talianko. "The people are good and I agree with the philosophy. The animals are incredible – it's great to get up close with the different species."

Four Vets: Dr. PJ Deitschel, Shirley Walter, Robyn Johnson, and Dr. Amber McNamara

How To Help Wild Animals

Mammals, birds, and reptiles are run over each day in the United States at a rate of one every 11.5 seconds. If you see an injured animal, please stop to help. Many species can live for days after being hit by a vehicle. Rat poison, glue traps and insecticides are responsible for many sick wildlife patients. Please be aware of unintended consequences of "pest control" and consider humane or eco-friendly products.

Nationally more than 7.8 million songbirds are killed each year by cats. Nearly 10% of CROW's patients are injured by domestic cats. To help wildlife, please make your feline a happy house cat.

Fishing line (monofilament) lasts up to 600 years. Fishing hooks do not pass harmlessly through the intestines of birds and marine mammals. If you don't fish, please educate someone who does – take your trash with you!

If a bird grabs your bait when you are fishing, or if you accidentally hook a bird, follow these steps:

1. Reel the bird in slowly.

2. If in a boat, use a landing net and boat the bird.

3. If on a pier, walk the bird to shore gently.

4. Cover the bird's head with shirt or towel to calm him.

5. For pelicans, egrets or herons, hold the middle of the bill with one hand and place your other arm over the bird's back and around his wings.

6. Carry the bird to get help. It may take more than one person to rescue the bird.

7. Cut the line close to the hook to get all monofilament off wings, legs, and body.

8. Place bird in a large box or wrap in towel and bring him to CROW or the nearest wildlife clinic.

9. If you are unable to contain or transport the bird, please call CROW at 239-472-3644 or call the nearest wildlife clinic.

The release is frequently the highlight for students and volunteers

*Great Quotes
About Wildlife*

All beings seek for happiness
— *Mahavamsa*

Northern Gannet

Northern Gannet

Eastern Screech Owl

Burrowing Owl

Burrowing Owl

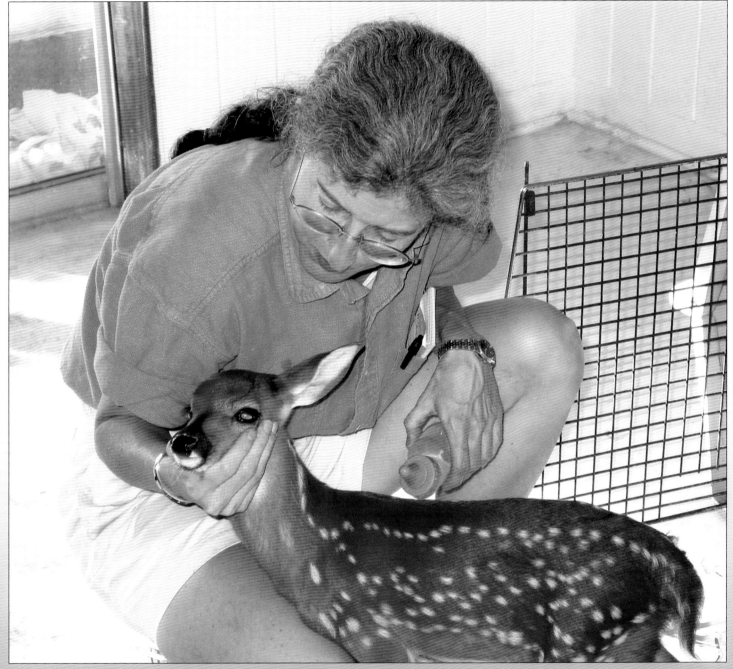

Dr. PJ with fawn

Ethics is
nothing else
than reverence
for life

— *Albert*
Schweitzer

They too are created by the same loving hand of God that created us

— *Mother Teresa*

Eastern Screech Owls

Animals are such
agreeable friends –
they ask
no questions,
they pass
no criticisms

— *George Eliot*

Dr. PJ with a wild pig

We consider all our animals to be our kids
— *Eric Roberts*

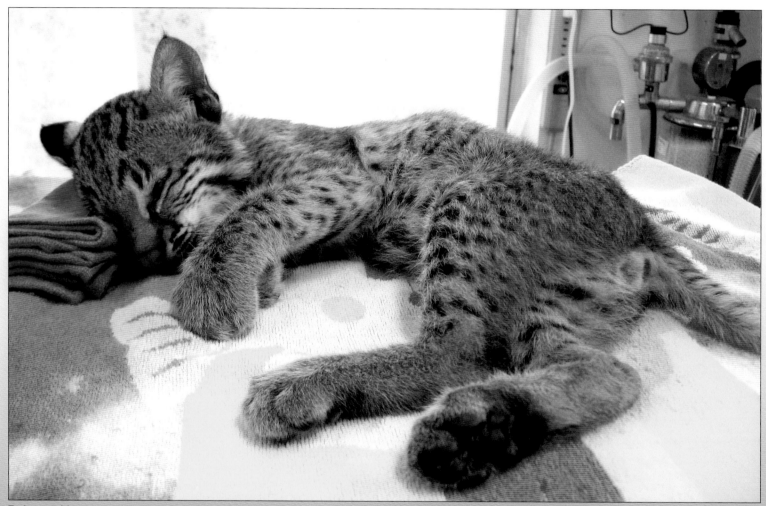

Bobcat taking a nap in surgery room

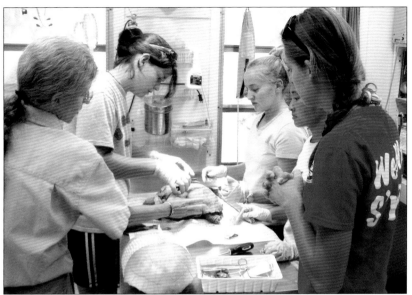
Dr. PJ instructs CROW students on repairing a turtle's carapace

The greatness of a nation...
can be judged by the way its animals are treated
— *Mahatma Gandhi*

Snowy Plovers

Loggerhead Sea Turtle carried from 900-gallon salt water tank

Animals possess souls
—*Pope John Paul II*

Gopher Tortoise

We preach love
and compassion for
all living creatures

— *Dali Lama*

Black Racer

American Alligator

Gopher Tortoise

Eastern Screech Owls

The love for all living creatures is the noblest attribute of man

—*Charles Darwin*

Yellow-Crowned Night Herons

Wild Hog

I like pigs.
Dogs look up to us.
Cats look down on us.
Pigs treat us as equals.

— *Winston Churchill*

About the Author

Brian Johnson writes the CROW
"Case of the Week" column for the
Island Sun Newspaper, and is a
Realtor for VIP Realty Group.
He has been on Sanibel since 1998.

Least Tern assists staff with an ID question

CROW Donation Information:

P.O. Box 150

Sanibel, Florida 33957

Crowclinic.org

(239) 472-3644

Bobcat release